My BIG Blended Family

APRIL MATA LOVATO

AuthorHouse™
1663 Liberty Drive
Bloomington, IN 47403
www.authorhouse.com
Phone: 833-262-8899

This book is printed on acid-free paper.

ISBN: 978-1-6655-5991-1 (sc)
ISBN: 978-1-6655-5992-8 (e)

Print information available on the last page.

Published by AuthorHouse 05/26/2022

authorHOUSE®

Hi, my name is Christopher! I'm 9 years old and in many ways I'm just like you! I like to play outside and hang out with my big sister, brother and friends. We ride our bikes, hoverboards, scooters and skateboards or go play at the park down the street from my house!

I have lots of fun in the summer when on summer break. I like to swim, have water balloon fights and play catch! Playing catch is one of my favorite activities because, I want to be a football player when I grow up!

There are 2 big trees in my front yard they provide a lot of shade in the hot summer months but when fall comes...

We love to play in the leaves. We drink hot Cocoa and carve pumpkins!! Then we clean the seeds and roast them for a tasty snack. Do you like pumpkin seeds too?

Growing up my mom had 9 step and half siblings. Mom told me that she's glad she had them because they helped her to become the person she is today. If I counted my brothers and sisters others siblings I would have 8 other siblings. How many siblings do you have?

Mom had my sister and brother when she was still young and growing up herself. I guess things didn't work out with their dads so they had to go to court to arrange a schedule. This means my brother and sister celebrate the holidays with their dads and stepmom's families too. Do you have a step-parent?

For me it's a little different though! Mom and my dad got a divorce when I was three years old. I still have some memories from then but not many since I was so young. My dad had a lot going on so him and mom decided that he could see or talk to me whenever he wanted. Mom always tells me that he loves me very much, but I wish he would come visit me and take me for ice cream like he used to. I haven't seen him in a long time. Sometimes I think he must have forgot about me?

I used to get mad and say mean things to my mom. I told her it was her fault my dad left, but that was wrong of me. It made her cry and I know I should have never said that! I finally realized that the person I was mad at was my dad, not my mom, but I was taking it out on my mom. You see it's not right to take your feelings of anger or sadness out on someone else. Especially when the person you take it out on did nothing to hurt you. When I saw my mom crying, I felt bad, and I apologized to her.

I know that mom works hard and takes good care of me. I know she doesn't keep me from seeing my dad, but I guess he's just busy with his new family. I still have my mom and lots of other family that love me a lot! Some days when my sister and brother are at their dads' houses me and mom have fun days, we go fishing, ride scooters, go out to eat or just spending quality time together. Do you have fun days too?

Did I mention that I want to be a football player when I grow up? I love all sports, but football is my favorite! Mom takes me to practice twice a week and games on Saturday! I love game day because my grandma grandpa aunt Uncle and brother all come to chair me on! I also play basketball and just started boxing as well. Do you play any sports? Sometimes moms' friends and their families come to cheer me on as well! My sister would come to, but she usually works on the weekends. I know she would be there if she could.

Now that my sister is 18 and just graduated from high school, she works a lot, but we spend a lot more time together since she has her own truck and can come see me whenever she wants! We have so much fun together. Last week I got to go with her and her friends to see a monster truck rally! It was so much fun to see the big trucks doing cool tricks! She even bought me a toy and took me to eat afterwards! I love my sister, she's awesome! Mom even lets me and brother go hang out at sisters' dads house sometimes and we spend the night, and stay up late playing video games with her sisters on her dads' side! Mom doesn't get mad or try to keep us away from them either, she says kids need all the love they can get, as long they treat me and brother good over there, then that's all that matters!

Mom also lets me, and sister go to Brothers' dads' house to! They are nice people as well! They invite us camping and to go do fun stuff all the time! For holidays and birthdays', they buy me and sister gifts to! We play board games and have lots of fun with brothers' other siblings on his dads' side of the family! Plus, it gives mom time to herself. She doesn't mind sharing me because she knows they are my family to. I know Sometimes my mom and my brother's dad disagree on things with the schedule, but they always figure it out. Mom says we don't need to worry about it because we are kids and we need to be kids, it's not our responsibility to worry about grown up things! I get to spend time with my brother, so I guess that's all that really matters!

I also have my grandparents. I go visit them often. I love to go to grandma and grandpas house because they have a big house with ducks and chickens for pets. I love my ducks and my chickens! In the morning I get to go to the chicken coop and collect their eggs. We use the eggs to cook breakfast and bake cakes! Fresh eggs are so good! Do you like eggs for breakfast too?

I have many aunt's uncles and cousins as well! I love playing with my cousins at grandma's house. Sometimes we disagree on things but at the end of the day we are all family and love each other no matter what. One thing for certain is that we have a very large family! My great great grandparents had 16 children!! That's a lot of kids, but mom says back then having a large family was common. My great great grandparents had a big ranch, which our family still has to this day. The ranch has been passed down from generation to generation. We go visit the ranch when we can because it's about an hour drive from where we live, I love it there! We roast marshmallows over the campfire and sing! I especially love to catch lizards and garner snakes, which aren't poisonous. Its fun to spend time with family at our land!

We also have days when it's just my mom, brother sister and I. we go do lots of fun stuff like renting a paddle boat on the river walk, fishing, going out to eat, swimming, shopping, going to the movies, or just hanging out at home! Whatever we do it's always fun with family! Sometimes my brother sister and I argue but not to often? I guess its normal, but what's important is that when we make mistakes we own up to them and we apologize! Its important to recognize when we are in the wrong so that we can learn from our mistakes! Learning from our mistakes is apart of life! Don't get to down on yourself when you make mistakes either, Just make sure that you learn from them and don't repeat the mistakes!

Some days it's just my mom, my brother and I. we do fun stuff then to! Mom takes us to amusement parks and lots of other fun stuff! I love to ride rides and hang out with my bro and mom! It's awesome! We are very close with our mom, and we always try to be respectful towards each other because we love and appreciate one another and we know mom works hard to take good care of us! She is the best mom ever!

Its also important to help mom out around the house to! She makes sure we keep our rooms clean and pickup after ourselves to! We always have to do chores before we can go outside to play. That's the rule! I like helping mom around the house! It's fun because we put music on and get to work, then our house is clean which makes mom happy! Mom does a lot for us so it's important to show her we care to by doing our chores.

I'm in fourth grade now, and I love going to school! I ride my bike to school everyday, accept in the winter. We live in Colorado where it gets really cold in the winter. Mom drives me to school in the mornings and picks me up after school during winter months. Even though my school is only a few blocks away from our house, mom doesn't like me to walk in the cold. So we bundle up, scrape the snow off of our windshield, warm up the car and off to school we go! Does it snow where you live?

I cant forget to leave out my brother Baby Bobby and sister Izabella Rose who passed away when they were babies. It was really hard for my mom to lose two children, and her own brother Bobby as well! We still celebrate their birthdays though. When we go visit them it's nice because they are all next to each other. It is hard for all of us. We wonder what they would be like today but I know that they are in heaven and we will see them again someday! Till then they are our Angels!

My brother and I also recently lost our best friend Marcus tragically. It has been hard. Losing people we love is never easy, because we miss them and we just want to see them again! Mom tells me that when people come into our lives we take the memories and what we learned from them and we keep them alive by remembering the good things and talking about them, because its good to express our feelings. Its ok to cry and be sad to, but its important to be happy and still live life, We never forget, we just make them proud! Talking to other people helps to, because we will always miss and remember them! Have you ever lost someone you were close to?

Remember family can be anyone. Even if you don't have the same DNA it's the people who love and support us and make life happier.There are many kids all over the world that live with step parents, or grandparents, adopted parents, aunts and uncles, whoever? As long as there is love from the heart and respect, that is the key to it! Never be ashamed if your life isn't perfect because no one has a perfect life, you just never know what other people are going through. Showing kindness and empathy are the best things we can all do to make the world a better place!

Be kind to everyone and love those who love you we are all people and we all have pains or things we deal with in life. You never know someone else's pain, so be kind and love. Thank you for reading our story!

This book is dedicated to Marcus.

April Rose Mata, 37 year old single parent. April has a lot of experience with family courts and parenting. She represented herself (pro se) in most of her child custody cases with much success! She is also certified in love and logic parenting styles with numerous hours of parenting education and hands on experience as well! April also volunteers her time for United Parents for Children™ helping parents understand family courts better and provide emotional support to other parents who have custody cases, the main goal is to be able to work with the other parent with our children's best interest in mind!

April also designs shoes, her brand name is Adonna Vi. Her shoes are made in Italy with designs for every shoe lover in mind! Along with that April is also a contractor for special events and medical supplys! April doesnt like to define herself by just one thing, we all have many talents, so its important to always believe in yourself!

Of everything April attributes her biggest success is her children! Spending time with her kids is by far her most favorite thing to do in the world! No matter what family situation we are in, what matters most is love, showing love, giving love, and recieving love is the number one ingredient in family! Never give up on your dreams or yourself! Life isn't always going to be easy, we all go through things in life that are meant to teach us new things and make us better people! Always remember to focus on the good things in your life! Bad things happen to everyone and overcoming the bad is the best thing we can all do for ourselves! Believe in yourself, trust yourself and love yourself and you will always win! LOVE LIGHT POSITIVITY!

Printed in the United States
by Baker & Taylor Publisher Services